Table of Contents

INTRODUCTION

Hydroponic growing is catching up with many weed, flower and vegetable farmers from across the globe. It is both interesting and beautiful. It is also versatile as it comes with many growing methods. The method, which entails growing crops in water rather than in soil, is not really a very new concept as it dates back to 600 B.C. One of the most popular hydroponics farming is tower gardening where people grow crops in vertical gardens. The towers, which use water, nutrients and motorized pumps, are ideal for the growth of herbs, vegetables, weed, fruits and flowers among many other kinds of crops.

CHAPTER ONE

Hydroponics

Hydroponics is the art/science of growing plants in a soil-free environment. Historically, hydroponics isn't that new.

In fact, there are many ancient records of people using the concept of hydroponics to grow plants.

One such important record is the Hanging Gardens of Babylon, which is considered one of the Wonders of the Ancient World. In Babylon, they used gravel and stones to grow plants.

While the system is certainly more primitive than what we can create now using our own two hands, it's important to note that the underlying principles remain the same.

This hydroponics guide will give you a bird's eye view of how hydroponics works, how it actually grows plants and how you can start your own hydroponic system.

How Does Hydroponics Work?

Hydroponic culture is soil-less, meaning, the soil has been completely eliminated from the equation. In place of soil, the grower uses a circulation system and hydroponic media to distribute water, nutrients, and air to the plants.

The safest combination is the coconut coir plus perlite combo (50/50).

The perlite provides adequate water and air distribution to different kinds of plants and is even used in conventional soil planting setups to improve the yield of crops.

There are a couple of reasons why people are shifting to hydroponics:

1. A greenhouse can obviously allow more plants to grow than a conventional plot of land.

A layer of pipes can be fashioned in a way that you will be able to plant double or triple the number of plants because other layers are elevated.

2. Water pumps for NFT (nutrient film technique) setups are becoming cheaper and setting them up is a breeze.

You can also cut power costs by creating a hybrid solar setup. We will discuss this shortly.

3. There are many types of media to choose from aggregated clay, perlite, coconut coir, rockwool, molded sponges, etc.

These media can be combined or you can use different media depending on the type of crop you wish to plant.

Is Hydroponics Hard To Do?

The complexity of any system of growing plants depends on what types of plants you want to grow, how big you want your system to be and how efficient your system is.

Generally speaking, smaller systems are easier to maintain and we highly recommend that you start with small systems so you don't get overwhelmed.

People have been relying on hydroponics for a long time! Remember the last time you had cut flowers in the house? What did you do to sustain its life for a few days?

You probably poured water in a vase and put the cut flowers there. If you're a bit savvy, you may have also added a bit of plant food to the solution to lengthen the lifespan of the flowers a bit more.

That is hydroponics! You sustained the life of a plant using a soil-less system.

The vase is the system, the cut flower is the 'crop.'

A large hydroponic system would, of course, have more parts because it's meant to support the growth of a planet from germination to harvest time.

Why Use Hydroponics Instead of The Normal Soil Method?

For thousands of years, people have been relying on the land for agriculture. Why try hydroponics now? There are of course specific benefits that put this method of growing plants a cut above the rest.

1. Since plants will be growing in a closed, water-driven system, soil-borne pests will be eliminated.

The same applies to fungal infections and other diseases that are normally associated with growing plants on the soil.

Remember that soil is essentially a miniature ecosystem of its own, with bacteria, fungi, and insects comprising its food web.

When you introduce a plant to the equation, the plant usually becomes either food or home. Either way, it's not good news for the plant!

2. A hydroponic setup eliminates the growth of unwanted plants (weeds) around your plants, eliminating the need to apply herbicides. This will radically reduce the amount of work needed to maintain your crops over time.

3. Since herbicides and other chemicals normally used to control both plant and animal pests are eliminated, the hydroponic farmer's health is also safeguarded.

Apart from measuring and mixing the nutrient solution, harmful chemicals will not be part of the maintenance equation. There are also natural ways to ward off even the tiniest of pests, such as the use of fine screens to prevent entry into the growing tent.

4. The turnaround time between planting is greatly reduced because the hydroponic system can easily be adjusted to match the requirements of the current planting project, as opposed to the preparation needed to make soil ready for planting.

Soil preparation involves the application of various types of nutrients before the soil can be even considered viable for certain crops.

In a hydroponic system, the circulated water (also known as the nutrient soup/stock) can be chemically analyzed and measured at any point to ensure that the chemical balance is just right for new planting.

5. And finally, the maturation cycle of crops can often be reduced (in other words crops grow faster) as the nutrient solution can deliver an ideal mix of nutrients over a period of time.

Ideal conditions are almost never attained by soil alone; it's different when you're dealing with a circulating system.

The Roots of A Plant Growing Through Hydroponics

The life of a plant in a hydroponic setup is dependent on healthy roots.

It is the only contact the plant has with the nutrient solution, and maintaining healthy roots is an utmost priority. One of the best ways to keep hydroponic plant roots healthy is ensuring they are oxygenated sufficiently.

When the roots of any plant (whether in a soil or soil-less environment) suffers from low or no oxygen conditions, the roots will shrivel up and die.

Water stagnation is another issue that needs to be addressed ASAP. A hydroponic system may be closed, but the water is still circulating, allowing the water to interact with the environment and exchange gas molecules with it (like the water in an aquarium with a pump!).

When you begin hydroponic culture, you will likely need to transplant seedlings from a smaller hydroponic setup to the main system.

Transplant shock happens when the roots of the transplanted plants die upon removal. The trick is to perform the transplantation slowly and surely. Don't rush the process – keep those fragile root hairs alive.

Also, keep the roots moist at all times. However, this shouldn't give you any wrong ideas: while the fragile root hairs of crops need to be kept moist, these can also suffer from being submerged in stagnant water, too.

Why? Stagnant water has low or no diffusible oxygen and the only way the roots can gain oxygen from its environment is by taking in pure elements.

Therefore, pure gaseous oxygen is required by the roots to remain alive throughout the transplantation process.

What Are The Different Types of Hydroponic Systems

Aeroponics

– Aeroponics is a radical new way of using the concepts of hydroponics to the fullest. Instead of submerging the root mat in water, the roots of plants are misted with nutrient solution at specific intervals.

– The misting provides high dissolved oxygen and nutrients to the roots of the plants, and since the plants are suspended in mid-air, the oxygen zone is continually exposed to plenty of air.

Water and nutrients that are not utilized by the plants are drained back easily to a trough below, preserving the nutrient solution for recirculation and continuous misting.

– The major challenge of this system is, it is highly reliant on the misting system. The roots of plants need to be continually moist.

When moisture disappears, the roots will soon shrivel up and die. When the pump and mist malfunction, the hydroponic grower needs to make sure that there is a backup mechanism that can continue the task of spraying/misting.

– The big upside of this system is the crop yield. Scientifically, crops that have been grown using the aeroponic system can produce yields that are ten times larger than what conventional soil systems and soil-free systems can produce.

This is a massive figure and we owe all this to the fact that aeroponics provides much higher oxygenation to the plant roots than other systems.

Pro Tip: A misting system needs a backup system too. A second smaller misting system can be put in place, or make sure that the roots of the plants can be lowered to a deep reservoir in the event of a power failure, in the event that you've decided to use an aeroponic setup.

– One of the solutions to pump failure is the introduction of a reservoir in the event of emergencies.

A reservoir can help maintain moisture and nutrient levels at acceptable degrees until the main pumps are brought back online.

Nutrient Film Technique (NFT)

– The NFT is the most accessible hydroponic system because all you need to set it up are pipes, a framework to hold up the pipes, a small pump and a small reservoir for the nutrient solution.

– NFT is highly recommended for beginners due to its ease of construction and its relatively high success rate for most types of vegetables.

– If you're using only a single frame with three to four pipes, you will only need a small, motorized pump to recirculate water throughout the system.

The natural drainage system will distribute nutrients to all parts of the system.

Growth rates will remain excellent and additional nutrients can be added as needed.

The nutrient film technique is an innovation by Allen Cooper at the Glasshouse Crops Research Institute in England.

In a nutshell, the system utilizes a closed, recirculating dynamic that continually runs the nutrient solution through enclosed pipes.

The plants are placed in intervals along the pipes, with roots reaching downward, toward the nutrient film. The pipes are interconnected, with the topmost pipe draining toward the second one below, and so forth.

There is natural aeration inside the pipes (as the pipes are not completely filled with water), plus, humidity is controlled as there are no additional openings in the pipes apart from the holes where the actual plants are situated.

Humidity control is important as the last thing that we want to do is to dry out the roots of plants. The oxygen zone has to be minded, but too much air can kill plants, too.

PRO TIP: Assess electrical equipment daily to ensure that water and air are being circulated adequately. Damaged equipment can easily lead to crop die-off.

Eventually, water is drained back to the main reservoir where an electrical pump recirculates the contents back to the system.

The challenge of the nutrient film technique is when plants begin to mature and the roots begin to form massive nets or mats that reach all the way down to the bottom of the narrow pipes.

The large root mats can result in water stagnation, which may eventually lead to root dieback.

Despite its shortcomings, NFT is rated as excellent in the hydroponic industry because of its ability to retain the nutrient solution (almost no evaporation happens because of the closed system).

Hydroponics Raft System (Deep Water Culture)

— Hydroponic rafts are highly recommended for crops that have low stature, like lettuce and other mixed greens.

If you're planning to plant large volumes of these crops, I highly recommend the raft system.

Hydroponics raft system is also referred to as deep water culture.

How Does The Raft System Work?

Essentially, you have a pool of nutrient solution in a low-depth, artificial pond.

Styrofoam sheets are placed on top, with small baskets placed in holes cut into the Styrofoam sheets.

Plants go into the small baskets and the medium is submerged in the nutrient solution.

How Can We Prevent Stagnation?

Obviously, a small pond doesn't flow (as with real-life ponds). The pool of nutrient solution is connected to a drain and pump that recirculates water continually, keeping the water in the small pool rich in plant nutrients and dissolved oxygen.

The water is renewed from below, and the plants thrive on having high dissolved oxygen and a constant influx of plant nutrients. Stagnation is avoided.

– The raft method is very economical and thus, a favorite of growers who are looking to harvest 2-3 times their normal yield when they plant their low-stature crops on the regular soil.

A hydroponic system is considered of high efficiency and value when it has achieved the following conditions:

1. The overall design is simple, easy to implement and relatively inexpensive.

2. Has been set up to be fully automated; the grower only needs to measure the nutrient solution and add water/nutrients as needed.

3. Maintenance is almost non-existence; the system takes care of itself 99% of the time.

4. Has been geared to support the type of plants that you want to grow in it in the first place.

For example, if your goal is to raise short-stature crops, your goal is to create an ideal raft system, because the raft system is appropriate for short-stature crops.

5. Does not waste the nutrient solution, or wastage is greatly reduced.

Any reduction in nutrient levels arises from the consumption of the plants themselves.

6. And finally, delivers the right combination of water, air, and nutrients so that your crops will not just survive, but thrive greatly in the hydroponic system.

What Are The Different Types of Hydroponic Media

• Coconut Coir

• Agricultural-Grade Perlite

• Clay Aggregate (LECA)

• Molded Sponges

• Rockwool

Note: You will see different names used for some of these. For example, Clay Aggregate is referred to as clay pebbles a lot of times. Just an fyi to help prevent any confusion.

This is one of the fascinating things about hydroponics. Yes, your plants will be growing in a soil-free environment. However, your plants still need a medium to anchor and grow on.

The medium or substrate will be replacing the soil that plants normally grow on. Another important function of hydroponic media is holding on to both water and air.

Roots need to be oxygenated and are only able to absorb pure elements when in contact with water. Early hydroponic systems made us of stones and sand.

Modern hydroponic systems have gone a long, long way and modern soil-less systems have now exceeded the performance of conventional growing setups for years now.

Your medium of choice is an important consideration if you want to profit from your hydroponic system.

Why is sand a generally bad idea for hydroponic systems? Plants can anchor on to it, right? The problem is with the interstitial spaces between the granules of sand.

Fine sand can't hold on to water and air efficiently. Large gravel, on the other hand, provides larger interstitial spaces for air and water, but unless your system recirculates the nutrient solution continually, water just passes through the large gaps between gravel particles.

Four of the most commonly-used media for hydroponic systems include:

– Coconut coir

– Agricultural-grade perlite

– Clay pellets

– Gravel

You may use any of these media types to get started. I personally recommend mixing equal parts of coconut coir and agricultural-grade perlite to vastly improve the water and air holding capacity of coconut coir.

If this doesn't work, feel free to try other combinations. There's a reason why these four media types are well-loved by hydroponic growers around the world!

Understanding The Differences Between These Mediums

Coconut Coir

We thought that coconuts are only fascinating because of their juice and 'meat.' Turns out, the emptied husk of the ever-versatile coconut is one of the perfect media to ever hit the hydroponic industry.

— Coconut coir is rich in natural plant hormones, naturally resists fungal infestations and allows the healthy spread of the finest root hairs.

— The fibers of the coconut husk are naturally resistant to sun exposure as coconuts have evolved through millions of years to survive being floated on the ocean until they are carried away to a viable sandbar or island, where the coconut can finally germinate.

There's a reason why 'castaway islands' are always drawn with coconut trees. 'Castaway' coconut trees are real!

– The most popular type of coconut coir is the compressed briquette. Coconut coir briquettes need to be pre-soaked before use.

After opening, submerge your briquettes in at least one gallon of water.

You will know that the briquettes are ready for use when a single briquette expands to up to six times its original size. The physical expansion is what we're after – it means that medium can hold a lot of air and water.

– Another fun fact about coir: it's not messy to use at all! If you get fibers on your clothes, all you need is to brush it off. Your hands will stay clean while handling it, too!

PRO TIP: Mix 50% perlite and 50% coconut coir to increase medium permanence.

Agricultural-Grade Perlite

Agricultural-grade perlite is one of the oldest media used for hydroponics. It is widely available, light, with a physical structure that makes hydroponic gardening a joy.

– Perlite also has high permanence, which means it can grab hold of nutrients, water, and air and maintain its hold on these three until the plant roots require them. This makes agricultural-grade perlite very root-friendly, indeed.

– Is often combined with soil to improve the growth rate of plants (imagine – it helps soil!)

– Perlite is also sterile and can tolerate changes in nutrient broth chemistry. It resists fungi and weeds, which is a plus in closed systems with lots of water, where root dieback is a big issue/possibility.

– Due to the lightness of the material, agricultural-grade perlite is not appropriate in 'flood and flush' systems as it can be easily carried away by flowing water.

Pure perlite systems are also out of the question for outdoor systems as wind and rain will easily carry it away, too.

– So when is it a good idea to use perlite? Perlite's permanence and expansive capacity is something to consider. It can definitely deliver the kind of retention that will benefit most crop varieties.

But the fact that it can easily be carried away by water is problematic. So like I said earlier, 50% perlite plus 50% coconut coir is a done deal for beginning setups!

Clay Aggregate

Also known as LECA or lightweight expanded clay aggregate, this type of medium has moderate water and air retention is denser and heavier than agriculture-grade perlite and is widely use in hydroponic systems, too.

– What makes LECA ideal for hydroponics is its pH neutral status, which is quite important for maintaining a healthy system.

Checking the pH of the nutrient solution is imperative because long-term changes can 'burn' the roots of plants.

– Lava rocks appear to have the same qualities as LECA. There are two problems with lava rocks that make them inappropriate for hydroponic systems.

One, they are not pH neutral and two, they suffer from sedimentation (from erosion) over time and the tiny sediments can damage equipment. Broken equipment can kill plants!

Molded Sponges

Molded sponges are considered the 'miracle medium' of hydroponics.

– Manufactured from a combination of compost and polymer, molded sponges are especially useful for germinating seeds and preventing transplant shock.

– The structure of molded sponges not only hold water and air in perfect proportions but also guide the hair-like roots of germinating plants so that they 'seek' outward (the way they do in soil) instead of growing in mixed directions, which is the main problem that hydroponic farmers encounter when germinating seeds.

– Molded sponges like Perfect Starts are classified as organic media, these sponges will not disintegrate during transplantation and will not leave harmful sediments that can clog and damage delicate equipment.

Unlike perlite, molded sponges are adequate performers in all kinds of hydroponic systems.

Rockwool

Rockwool has been around as a hydroponics medium for about twenty years.

– It is manufactured from molten rock. Molten rock is spun into fibers, aggregated, and then re-compressed as bricks.

The resulting bricks can readily absorb water, air, and nutrients.

As the surface is porous, with viable interstitial spaces, water also drains decently.

– Rockwool is lauded because of its pH neutrality and being free of any pathogens that can harm seedlings and cuttings.

Large slabs of this material can be used for years to maintain large tracts of hydroponic crops.

– Rockwool is highly reusable. It can be reused for planting after steam-sterilization.

– One downside is that it produces a fine dust when first removed from its packaging.

This fine dust has been known to cause skin allergies, which has led me to believe that it may also cause respiratory issues if you happen to inhale large volumes of the dust. Caveat emptor, in this case.

The Different Types of Hydroponic Setups (Not Systems)

Now that you know the history and various media used to grow plants hydroponically, it's time to take a peek at the various hydroponic systems themselves.

Basic: Sand and Gravel Hydroponic System

Sand and gravel systems are considered the most basic, 'nitty-gritty' of all hydroponic systems.

Yes, plants can survive in this system but the fact remains that sand normally has poor aeration.

A sand and gravel system can be fed water and nutrients by a small air pump. As long as the nutrients are there, you'd be surprised at the type of media that plants will accept as growing media.

Think plants growing in cement cracks. Cement cracks are not ideal, but there are moisture and nutrients there, so some small plants find the cracks alright to grow in.

Now, when the roots of plants don't get sufficient air, poor aeration results. And this situation leads to... you guessed it right – root rot!

As I've mentioned before, maintaining pristine roots is essential for keeping crops healthy.

Why do plants need air 'down there?'

People generally attribute plant respiration to the leaves – and rightly so, because leaves do interact with all sorts of variables in the environment, not just air and moisture.

However, it turns out that the roots of plants also breathe! Yes, they respire 'down there.'

The roots are considered an 'oxygen zone,' too, which necessitates tilling and aerating the soil ever so often when plants are planted in soil.

When you're dealing with a hydroponic system, obviously, you can't just take a trowel and tamp on your substrate to improve aeration.

The medium has to be efficient on its own in providing sufficient surface area for respiratory exchange to occur between the roots and the water.

The Dutch Bucket Hydroponic System

Aptly named because the system was first used in Holland, the Dutch bucket system is one of the easiest systems to create and implement.

This system is appropriate for commercial growing setups for long-term crops such as tomatoes and cucumbers.

The hydroponic farmer is free to use any kind of medium, be it coconut coir, perlite, coir-perlite mix, rockwool, etc.

Here's how it works: the 'bucket' is actually a 2.5-gallon plastic container made of heavy-duty plastic.

It is recessed on one side so that it sits on top of a 1.5-inch pipe that serves as its flush or drain.

The recess raises the draining point of the bucket, leaving a reserve layer of water below.

This reserve layer is continually renewed as the bucket is fed new nutrient solution via a double drip. A quantity of solution is always available in the bucket (i.e. the Dutch bucket does not fully drain) in case something happens to the double-drip system and the buckets are left with no new water for a certain amount of time.

On the other hand, too much water in the bucket can cause stagnation, which is also bad for plant roots, thus, necessitating a continuous drain system that brings back the water to the main reservoir.

Rockwool Slab Drip Hydroponics System

Rockwool slabs are massive media for growing crops hydroponically.

These slabs are easy to install, easy to use and can be used to grow plans like tomatoes to full maturity and beyond. In fact, many commercial hydroponic growers use rockwool slabs to 'air layer' tomato plants so that the plants will extend to up to 40 feet in the air!

Strings are used to support the tomato vines, allowing the bottom of the vines to thrive while allowing for maximum growth.

The downside of the system, of course, is that there is a run-off.

Water being dripped onto the slabs will eventually percolate to the bottom of the slabs and drain away to the floor of the grow tent.

Proper drainage is necessary to prevent stagnant water from inundating the grow tent, especially if all of the plants are planted on rockwool slabs.

The Ein Gedi Hydroponics System

– The Ein Gedi system was developed in Ein Gedi, Israel.

– It is a hybrid system that does away from with the usual drip system.

– Instead of relying on the natural percolation of water to the root zone, what the Ein Gedi system does is it sprays or mists the roots of the plants.

The misting introduces such a high amount of dissolved oxygen to the roots that plants grow vigorously over a shorter period of time.

– What about the rest of the roots? As the root mat expands, it grows beyond the spray-able zone.

But no worries! Right below the spray zone is a small pool of nutrient solution that is also recirculated vigorously.

The nutrient-rich solution is also high dissolved oxygen and prevents stagnation and root dieback.

– The Ein Gedi system is fully enclosed. Imagine a box or frame, with fixed baskets inside.

A small pipe mists the spaces in between the plant baskets, introducing O2-rich and nutrient-rich water to the plant roots.

– This hydroponic system is highly recommended for growing healthy seedlings and growing cuttings.

Can be used indoors and is relatively easy to set up.

The main water reservoir is placed below the main frame of baskets and drainage is direct and easy to spot and measure.

What's The Best Way To Power Your Hydroponics System

Hydroponic systems require continuous power to run, especially if you're using a recirculating system to drive water to the plants and back to the main reservoir.

Obviously, the most reliable source of power would be an AC tap.

However, some people want to save power while reducing their overall carbon footprint.

How can you do this with your hydroponic setup?

The answer is solar power. A hybrid solar setup can run your greenhouse completely "off the grid" provided that you do things properly.

I will provide a basic rundown of the things you will need to create a solar set up that will run your greenhouse with the power of the sun completely, day and night.

For this project, you will need a solar or car battery (or batteries), appropriately-sized wires, a low-voltage DC breaker, solar panels (100 watts or more, depending on the electrical load), DC-AC inverter, voltage regulator and an SCC or solar charge controller.

WHICH SYSTEM WORKS BEST FOR YOU?

DRIP SYSTEM

Space

A basic drip system is achievable for any beginner. It will take up a little more room because there are two large containers. Ideally, the system could sit on a table.

Budget

There is more equipment to buy using this method. You will need at least one circulating pump, a timer, and tubing. You will also want a drip manifold. If the budget is tight, you can make small holes in the tubing instead. This system requires a growing medium.

It can be less expensive to run than the Water Culture, or Ebb and Flow, systems. This is because it makes more efficient use of the nutrients, therefore using less. This may not make much difference on a smaller garden. To benefit from this, you would need at least 10+ plants in the system.

Experience

It is a little complicated to set up. This method is more sophisticated than Water Culture, which can be done in a single bucket. It is also more complex than the Ebb and Flow to set up. If you are a beginner, it might be better to buy a ready-made kit that has all the right components in one place.

Be aware that tubing can become blocked with the excess minerals from the nutrient liquid. Be vigilant of this because your crop could soon dry up and die from not receiving any water.

A higher skill level is needed with this system. You need a basic understanding of balancing the concentration of nutrients. You also need a good knowledge of how often the pump should be on and off. Get these wrong and your plants will suffer. If it is not enough, then the roots could be stunted, or even worse, dry out. If it is too much, the roots could rot or grow a fungus.

This system relies on electrical power. Make sure you check it periodically and know what to do if it goes off.

Time

There are a few maintenance tasks that will require attention. The flow of nutrients should always be well balanced. Check the pipes often so they don't get blocked. Should the electricity cut off, the whole system will come to a stop. It is vital you check it often because you can lose your entire crop.

Each of these issues is very important to the success of your garden.

Failure on any of these points and your crop will die.

EBB AND FLOW

Space

Very similar in space requirements to the Drip System. The growing tray should be sitting on a table with the reservoir container underneath so it can make full use of gravity. This system works well indoors.

Budget

To set this system up, you will need to buy some basic equipment, such as a pump, tubing, timer and medium.

Experience

It is easy to maintain, once you get the hang of it. However, it can be a little complicated to set up. If

DIY is not your thing, then there are ready-made kits to buy containing everything you need.

Measuring temperature and pH levels is not quite so important with this method. You should still measure these levels however just not as often.

Time

Nutrient water in the reservoir will need changing every 7-10 days. Also, the system will need a thorough clean, with hydrogen peroxide, after a harvest. It is best to check pH levels daily so you can adjust them if needed. You need to check on a regular basis that the pump is working and the tubing does not become blocked.

NUTRIENT FILM TECHNIQUE

Space

The grow tray is usually a gulley or channel, so it can be lengthy. You also need space for a reservoir tank that holds the nutrient-enriched water. Again, it is better if the grow tray is situated on top and the reservoir below. Like many hydroponic systems, if it is kept small, it can be set up inside.

Budget

As it is a constant flow system, you will need a pump, but a timer is not necessary. It is an inexpensive way to start your hydroponic growing. However it is also a little complicated, so be aware. No medium is required.

The plants are held in baskets, in a lid with holes, so the roots hang out and reach the channel of water. To ensure the reservoir water is well aerated an air stone fed by an air circulating pump is a good option.

Experience

Setting up can be tricky. The grow channels need to be at an angle so the water runs down from one end to the other. If the angle is wrong, then the plants could flood or dry out. You will need to know how to measure pH and temperature levels because these need checking every day.

Time

NFT is easy to maintain with little work required to keep it working well. The biggest job is replacing the nutrient-enriched water. This needs to be done every two weeks to ensure the plants are correctly fed. After harvesting, your system will need a thorough clean out. Otherwise, the growing channel and reservoir will build up with harmful bacteria. Suspended roots can grow too long and restrict the flow of water. If this is the case, then you can trim them without harming the plants. It is important to keep the water temperatures cool, at around 68F/20C.

WATER CULTURE

Space

You could start with as little as the space required for a 5-gallon bucket.

Everything that you need can be comfortably confined to one container. It can become more elaborate if you wish to extend the system later. One bucket, nutrient water, and a lid with holes in it are all you need to get started on this hydroponic system. Unless you grow individual plants in pots, with the roots suspended in the nutritional water, then you don't even need a growing medium.

Budget

This can be the least expensive system to set up.

It can run without a medium by hanging your plants through a hole cut in a lid. It might be better to use small baskets for the roots so the plants have some means of support.

You will need to buy medium if you choose to use plant pots for each plant.

Unless you are running a larger system, you do not need a water pump.

If you start small with the one container, you can grow 1-4 plants in the same system. This is what I recommend for the beginner. Start small, then as you gain experience, expand your system.

Experience

Water Culture is one of the simplest growing systems. This means that it is easy to set up, even with a limited knowledge. Plants are fast growing in this system because their roots are in the nutritional liquid all the time.

No need to worry about researching and choosing the right medium, as it does not need any if you wish to keep it simple.

The main things to watch out for are:

Ensure the water temperature stays at a specific level, around 68F/20C, to maintain the oxygen and inhibit the growth of harmful bacteria. Keep the container in the shade a

Pnd out of direct sunlight, if you can. Paint the container white as this helps reflect the heat.

You will also need to keep your eye on the pH levels in the water.

You will need to change the nutrient-water every 10 days or so.

This is essential for keeping the nutrients at a prime level and stop the buildup of harmful chemicals.

Start with only one or two plants. As you gain confidence, add to the system.

You could add another bucket and introduce a recirculating garden, however, this needs a pump. The water pumps from one bucket to the next so all the buckets are not running on an individual system.

Time

It is simple to set up and can probably be achieved in half a day, depending on the size of your system.

Other than periodically checking the temperature and pH levels, the only time-consuming task will be changing the water. Each bucket must be given fresh water and nutrients.

You can cut down the time spent on this task by using a pump and the recirculating method. Basically, it means the water is pumped from one bucket to the next so all the buckets are not run individually but are using the same water. This way, when you do have to change the water, you only need to concentrate on the main bucket's solution mixture. You will still need to drain the whole system but the other buckets will soon fill up from your main bucket flow.

AEROPONICS

Space

Not ideal for a beginner as there are few "small" Aeroponic Systems. You do need lots of space to make this method worthwhile. Technically, you could do a small garden in a large tub with about six plants.

Budget

This is the most expensive system to set up. You are going to need the essentials, such as filters, tubes, and pumps. You MUST also use high-quality nutrients, as low-quality ones have more salt residue and are more likely to block the sprayers.

Experience

The most difficult for a beginner. However, it is probably the system that will yield the most harvest.

If you do things wrong, you WILL lose your entire crop.

Time

High maintenance or your crop will die.

Blockages

Needs regular checks that the sprayers do not clog up with minerals from the nutritional liquid. If unattended, the roots will dry up and the plants will die.

Temperature

Needs regular temperature checks and water should be at around 64F/18C.

Humidity

Needs constant checking and the levels can vary: i.e. vegetable or fruit stage should read 60-70%; flowering stage 30-40%. If it is too much, it will cause algae or rot, and too little will stunt growth or the roots will dry up.

Does have a speedy harvest cycle, so if run correctly, then the plants will grow fast.

WICK IRRIGATION

Space

Ideal if you have limited space, particularly if your hydroponic garden is to be indoors. Similar in size to the Water Culture System and crops can be grown in just one bucket.

Budget

A basic Wick System is one of the cheapest hydroponic methods you can use.

However, it does need a growing medium and a suitable fabric to use as the wick. For this system, you will need an absorbent growing medium, such as clay, perlite or coir. Plus, you still need to buy the nutrients.

The system would benefit from an aeration pump and air-stone. If the water is still, nutrients can sink to the bottom of the feeding reservoir.

Experience

Although a seemingly simple arrangement, the Wick System is not without its problems. It is easy to set up and get started. It is not very good for larger plants that need lots of water and nutrients. A novice should begin with smaller, quick-growing plants. If you are a beginner, stick to herbs or lettuces, because this system will be ideal for such crops.

The wick is important and you must use a material that will soak up liquid efficiently. Rope, fabric and felt are useful for this purpose. It may be a case of experimentation, trial, and error. If wicks do not work correctly, then the roots will dry up and the plants will die.

Time

As the wick and medium can become soaked in salt minerals, this system does need regular maintenance. Plants will only soak up the nutrients the need leaving behind all those they don't want. The minerals remain in the wick and medium and can build up. To counteract this, you will need to flush the medium with fresh, clear water, periodically. Plus, you will also need to top up the nutritional water reservoir.

If you don't use an air pump to create movement in the still water, you will need to stir up the reservoir water. Do this at least a couple of times a day

Framework For Setting Up A Solar Panel For Your Hydroponics System

1. Set up your solar panels securely. Make sure that your frames are properly angled so that your solar panels will catch the maximum amount of UV rays from the sun.

Do not position your solar panels under a tree.

Full exposure to the sun is necessary. Shade can vastly reduce the available power to your solar panels, reducing the efficiency of your solar setup.

2. Connect your solar panel to your low voltage breakers. Make sure that you are connecting the wires from your solar panels to LOW VOLTAGE DC BREAKERS.

Setting up anything electrical (including solar panels) can be dangerous. We recommend either hiring an electrician or doing thorough research if you decide to do it yourself.

These are different from your usual 5 amp or 15 amp AC circuit breakers.

DC breakers are designed to respond to short-circuits resulting from very low voltages (10 volts or less) whereas AC circuit breakers expect voltages of at least 100 volts in order to function normally.

The task of low voltage DC breakers is to make sure that the line coming in from the solar panels, in the event of an electrical catastrophe, does not burn the entire setup.

3. Connect your SCC to the solar battery or car battery. Large-capacity car/truck batteries are perfect for hybrid solar setups.

The capacity of a battery is measure in amp-hours.

DC batteries come in a variety of voltages; solar setups normally use 12-volt batteries or 24-volt batteries.

Larger-capacity 24-volt batteries are more expensive but last longer and provide more power over the period of a day.

4. Connect your battery to the DC-AC inverter. The job of the inverter is to convert direct current (DC) from the battery to alternating current (AC) which can be used by equipment and appliances running on AC power. Household appliances run on AC power.

5. Connect the inverter to your power regulator. Your power regulator will serve as a breaker, too.

In the event of a short circuit, the power regulator's fuse will blow, which should help protect against fires that may result from shorted wires.

If you're up for it, you may install a separate circuit breaker and plug your voltage regulator to that too. The AC circuit breaker will protect the line going to the inverter.

Optional: you may connect your power regulator to a multi-tap extension setup.

I highly recommend using only heavy duty extension taps with built-in circuit breaking mechanisms.

Normally these taps have a reset button. Lightning-protect taps are also highly-prized as greenhouses can be hit by lightning.

A lightning-protect tap will switch itself off in the event of an extreme power surge, saving your equipment from instant damage.

Your new setup will function this way:

1. In the morning, your greenhouse will be feeding off the sun's power as the sun will continually recharge the battery.

2. At night, your battery/batteries will have a full charge, which means your greenhouse will continue running on battery charge alone until

morning comes and your battery starts charging again.

3. Since there are plenty of safety measure installed, the solar setup will be safe and operate on autopilot.

Just make sure that in the morning you check the readings on each part of the system so that you know that your setup is working normally.

Pro Tip: Create a backup power source for your hydroponics system so that you can save your crops in the event of hours or days-long power failure.

CHAPTER TWO

Hydroponic-Tower

The system takes very little space, which is one of the reasons people like it, the towers come with several residential units that house the crops. Majority of hydroponic towers are portable, compact, efficient and very easy to use. If you are thinking that because they are towers ad cannot produce as much as growing crops on the ground would, you are wrong because this method of farming gives just as much produce as the soil or other methods would. Sometimes the yields are even better and the crops look healthier.

Besides the high yields, HYDROPONIC TOWER growing transforms the place to look beautiful and to smell nice because of the rich foliage of the crops. Mostly used outdoors within the home compound, hydroponic towers stand upright and tall which makes it easier to monitor the crops and to harvest. Below we look at some of the best hydroponic towers in the market.

Stacky Large 5 Tier Vertical Garden Tower

Large 5 Tier Vertical Garden Tower - 5 Black Stackable Indoor / Outdoor Hydroponic and Aquaponic Planters (24 Quart Tower - 13x13x26)

Mr Stacky is one of the leading manufacturers of gardening towers. The large 5-tier vertical tower comprises of s black stackable hydroponic planters made with durable food safe polypropylene material. The tower designed for both indoor and outdoor use keeps the roots shielded from light and algae from getting into the plants. The 24 QRT tower measurements vary between 12x12x25 and 13x13x26. It has a flow through design that protects the plants from over watering diseases and root rot.

Grow up HGTC Vertical Hydrogarden Deluxe Planter Kit

For people that want to have a vertical garden without the need of an automatic timer on their system, then they can use the quality HGTC Vertical Hydrogarden Deluxe Planter Kit by Grow up. The kit uses only 4sq ft. of the space you have set aside and it can grow up to 20 plants. The hydroponic kit works well both indoors and outdoors. Included in the kit is a submersible pump, 5 stackable gardening pots, plumbing, reinforced lid, 20-gallon reservoir and 4 9-litter bags of growing medium.

The kit also includes 1 QTR. of nutrients to help with the drop growth. Benefits of the Vertical

Deluxe Planter Kit are you will never have to worry about weeding your plants, no pests, you can grow your crops in doors and not worry about any mess, you can plant all year round and it occupies very little space, it is easy to assemble and it is very affordable. The kit is compact and portable and it comes with everything you need for 20 plants.

Mr. Stacky 5-Tier Stackable Vertical Gardening Indoor/Outdoor Tower

Many of the vertical gardening towers use soil for growing crop but there are few vertical towers for hydroponic gardening and one such good example is Mr. Stacky 5-Tier Vertical Gardening Tower. The only difference and something you need to take into serious consideration is that some of the hydroponic vertical towers do not come with timers or pumps therefore they need skill to grow the crops.

The tower, made from food safe polypropylene saves water, space and allows for efficient growth of your hydroponics plants. You can use it both indoors and outdoors and it is ideal for crops such as herbs, flowers, vegetables and weed among others. On each layer of the tower, is a water reservoir which makes it even easier to grow your crops because there will be no crop over-watering. The tower includes 5 stackers with 20 planting locations and a bottom drip tray that ensures the place stays messy free.

Garden Tower 2

Have fun growing your weed in a self-contained system that comes with other amazing benefits. I am talking about the revolutionary vertical self-contained garden tower, which takes home gardening to a completely new level. The system, which uses potting soil rich in nutrients, enables the plants to grow efficiently looking healthy with more yields. You can plant up to 50 weed plants or any other plants you wish to plant vertically in a minimal footprint.

This method of growing the plants eliminates weeding loss of nutrients and use of electricity power. The system also ensures that there is no water loss commonly associated with conventional gardening methods. The tower occupies 4 square feet of the space provided and vermin composting fuels the growth of the crops. By using this tower, you will harvest fresh food free from PVC, BPA, Polycarbonates, Phthalates, Pesticides, Herbicides and many other contaminants. The eco-friendly gardening tower is eco-friendly and saves you tons of money.

Foody Hydroponic Vegetable Support Tower

Grow your favourite crops hydroponically indoors without worrying about them lacking anything. Besides harvesting the freshest and most healthy looking crops, indoor gardening also adds a certain beauty to the room because of the foliage and the crop aromas. One of the best systems to use for indoor hydroponics gardening is the Foody Vegetable Support Tower. The system is ideal for climbing plants such as cucumbers, tomatoes lentils, beans, herbs and okra among many others.

It is also great for other crops such as cannabis lettuce, cabbage and spinach among many others. The system comes with an in built automatic water level sensor that softly chimes when the level is low. You can grow your crops in the medium form scratch or transport seedling to continue growing there. The system occupies a space floor of 8"by 20" and its height is only 40" inches tall. The complete kit includes a growing medium, climbing frame, and fertilizer. It is easy to set up and just as easy to use.

Huge Greenstalk 5 Tier Garden Planter

This soil patented vertical garden made in east Tennessee comes with 30 planting pockets that you can use to plant various crops. You can use the tier for vegetables flowers, herbs, some fruits such as strawberries and weed. You can also plant larger crops like zucchini, tomatoes, peppers and corn. Made from high quality UV-resistant and thick PVC free plastic, the 5-tier garden planter is portable, maximises your garden, adds height and beauty to your room space and is easy to use. You can use the planter as a tower as a stack or a non-stack.

You do not have to worry about the infestation of pests or over watering your crops. Every tier holds a cubic foot of potting mix and each tier comes with 12 drainage holes. You can also use the planter for organic gardening. Included in the system are 5 planters each with 6 planting pockets, 4 grey watering disks, an instructions manual, and 1 top water reservoir. Use POTTING SOIL for your gardening for best results.

You want to have stress free gardening, just fill up your greenstalk 5-tier garden planter with water and watch as the water flows from the top reservoir distributing water equally in every tier as it feeds your crops. The texture of the soil will tell you when you need to add more water. The tower is durable and crack free.

Factors to consider when buying a tower garden

A tower garden comes in very handy especially when you have limited space and want to plant as many plants as you possibly could. The market has a variety of hydroponics tower gardens and it is essential to understand what you want for efficient gardening. Below are some of the factors to consider before you go buying your next tower garden.

Materials

The material of the tower garden is very important as it contributes to the wellbeing of the plants. A good tower garden is made from BPA-free and UV stabilised material. The material should be high quality food safe plastic, compliant with the FDA guidelines. The best hydroponics tower has an opaque material that keeps the light from penetrating into the plant roots and the soil or water. This ensures that no algae gets inside the planters, keeping the plants happier, healthier, fresh and clean at all times during their growing period. A good material also ensures that your tower planter enjoys a longer life and many seasons of growing your best crops.

Dimensions

Depending on the space available and the amount of crops you want to grow, you should take the dimensions of the tower seriously. Majority of the towers occupy space floors not exceeding 6sq. ft. some also come with reservoirs that hold 20 gallons of water and stand at anything from 20 inches to over 80 inches tall if it has an extension kit. The taller the tier, the more plants it can hold. You can have as many towers as you want in a very limited space.

Number of plants you want to grow

The number of plants you want to grow will also determine the kind of tower planter you will buy. Majority of the tower plants come with pockets for 29 plants. Others have pockets for 30 plants while those with extensions can accommodate over 80 plants. If you want more than 20, you will need to buy a larger tower planter; several tower planters or you get an extension for your tower planter.

What you want to grow

The good thing with hydroponics tower gardens is that you can plant anything you choose to plant apart from root crops. the kind of crops that do well with tower gardens are herbs weed, strawberries, vegetables, tomatoes and flowers among many others. Knowing what you want your vertical tower for will help you in choosing the correct one.

Ease of use and set up

A vertical tower should come with an easy set up that anyone can use with ease. Check if the tower comes with a timer in case you are using glow lights and check if the hydration system is okay. A good tower should be cost effective and use as little electricity as possible saving you on monthly bills. The accompaniments should also make the tower user friendly so make sure your planter has all the things it should have for growing your crops. These may include water reservoirs, number of pockets, automatic water level sensors, bottom drip trays and number of stackers. Majority of the vertical hydroponic towers also come with nutrients on purchase.

Design

Majority of the vertical tower planters do well either indoors or outdoors. If you are going to use your tower indoors, make sure you go for an attractive design that will compliment your home furnishings and deco. An elegant tower adds to the beauty of the home and once the crops foliage starts sprouting, the whole place gets a new transformation.

Things to consider before you start vertical gardening

Once you have your vertical tower, you should consider the following factors before you start growing.

Temperature for growing your hydroponics

Light should be sufficient for the proper growth of the crops

Nutrients for those vertical towers that do not come with them on purchase

Grow mediums that act as support for the plants root system while at the same time providing aeration and good drainage

The space where the crops will grow should have sufficient airflow both indoors and outdoors. With the indoors plants, you can use fans to help maintain good airflow in the room. Some of the most advanced vertical towers have their own oxygenating features.

Different kinds of plants need different pH levels to control their acid levels. It is therefore necessary to have adjusters ready to check the levels before you start your hydroponics growing.

Wrapping it up

Choosing the best vertical hydroponics tower for your growing is not hard if you know what you want. VERTICAL HYDROPONICS towers come with many benefits and they make farming fun and stress free. Hydroponic growing has faster growth of crops as compared to other conventional methods of farming. What is even better is that majority of the towers are compact and portable and you can enjoy the yields from the crops as well as the beauty they add to your home space. We hope this article was helpful and with the products named above, you will enjoy vertical hydroponics tower gardening.

HYDROPONIC TOWERS, WHAT'S THE DEAL?

Vertical gardening, also referred as "hydroponic tower," "hydroponic grow system," "Tower garden" or hydroponic "vertical garden" are hydroponic systems that allow horticulturists to grow all kind of plants in a well-organized vertical structure.

In other words, vertical grow towers are hydroponic systems that utilize motorized pumps, water, and hydroponic nutrient solution to grow herbs, fruits and any other type of plant. Each system has numerous "residential units," which are essentially the holes on the sides of the system which house each plant.

The towers stand upright, are compact, portable, easy to use, and are extremely efficient. For their square footage, it is quite amazing how much produce each tower can yield.

Building a Vertical Hydroponic Tower

Hydroponics is a method of growing plants without soil in a horizontal or vertical fashion, where mineral nutrients are provided through the water. Hydroponic systems that allow growing of plants in a vertical fashion are known as vertical hydroponics. Vertical hydroponics works by using conventional hydroponic techniques in a vertical, gravity fed system. The nutrient-rich water is fed from the top and collected at the bottom.

Vertical hydroponics has various advantages over traditional crop production methods including:

Allows for high density yield per unit area.

Good for small sunny places like balconies, patios and rooftops.

It allows year around production inside.

It often can provide more than 90 percent efficiency in water use.

No soil-borne diseases.

Tower Garden

Material required

One white vinyl fence post 5 inches x 5 inches x 8 feet

Two white vinyl pyramid post tops

One 45-gallon tank

A plastic sheet for preparing a lid for the tank, which provides support to the tower and should be opaque to avoid growth of algae.

3-inch PVC pipe (10 feet)

Submersible pump (400 gallons per hour) with attachments

Light timer

5/8-inch x 5/8-inch x 8-foot white vinyl blind stop molding – cut into 12 4-inch pieces.

Spray adhesive

PVC epoxy

28 3-inch net pots

One silver 1-inch narrow utility hinge

Two brass 1 ½-inch narrow utility hinges

Eight #6 32-inch x 3/8-inch machine screws with nuts

Clear silicone for aquariums

½-inch nylon hose barb tee

10-foot length vinyl hose inner diameter ½ inch – outer diameter – 3/4 inch

4-inch x 24-inch aluminum pipe for dryer vents

Medium grit sandpaper

Tools needed

Miter saw

Tape measure

Ruler

Drill

Various drill bits:

1/2-inch for cut out pilot hole and also for tee barb

5/32-inch hole for hinges

1/8-inch holes for water tray

Jig saw with fine blade

Soldering iron

Two U clamps (1/4-inch x 3/4-inch x 2-1/2-inches)

Steps for building tower

Take a white vinyl fence post 5-inch x 5-inch x 8-foot and cut according to the height wanted for the tower. The recommended height for a vertical towers is 5 to 6 feet, which is easily accessible by most people.

Drill a hole in the plastic sheet used to prepare the lid to allow the fence post (tower) through it using the square template listed under template links on the last page.

Place the net pot hole template on the tower at the spacing according to the crop to be grown in the tower. Stagger the holes on each side so the pots do not touch each other inside the tower.

Paste the pot hole template on the fence post using adhesive.

Drill a hole at one end of the template so the jig saw can work.

Using the jig saw, cut a pot hole of the same size as the template.

Take a 3-inch PVC pipe and cut at a 45-degree angle with a height of 2.25-inches. This will prepare the net pot support (Figure 2). This is suitable for 3-inch net pots, but if net pot size is changed in the tower, then the pot hole size and net pot support will need to be modified.

Net pot support.

Make a rectangular cut at the bottom of the tower using a template for the holes at the bottom of the tower. This will allow the water supplied from the top to exit.

Place the net pot holder on the bottom of the net pot hole on the tower. Rub the area with sand paper where the net pot holder needs to be glued. Use the PVC epoxy on the edge of the net pot holder and place it on the bottom of net pot hole with some weight on it and let it set for two to three hours. Fix all the net pot holders throughout the length of the tower.

Prepare the top of the tower by using two white vinyl pyramid post tops. Drill a ½-inch hole through the center of the top and pass a ½-inch tee barb to supply nutrient solution to the tower.

Use the other white vinyl pyramid post top to drill the holes on all sides to distribute nutrient solution throughout the tower. Approximately 10 random holes should be drilled (Figure 3).

Vinyl pyramid post top with holes.

Attach both white vinyl pyramid post tops by using the hinge. On the opposite side, attach the top with holes to the tower using the other hinge and cover the screws with clear silicone for aquariums to avoid corrosion (Figure 4).

Both white vinyl pyramid post tops attached to tower.

Take a 5/8-inchx 5/8-inch x 8-foot white vinyl blind stop molding and cut into 12 4-inch pieces. Rub the side of this piece with sand paper, which needs to be attach inside of the tower. Also, rub the inside of tower above each net pot hole. Apply PVC epoxy on the rubbed edge and place it inside the tower. This will help in proper distribution of the nutrient solution through the tower.

Place the net pot in a net pot hole and mark the edges, which touch the top of the net pot hole. Melt this area with a soldering iron. This will prevent flow of water along the edge of pot outside of the tower and also facilitate easy placement of the pot into the hole.

On the covering of the reservoir, cut out a piece to make a small lid that is attached by a hinge. Apply clear silicone for aquariums to avoid the corrosion of the screws. This will facilitate adding of nutrient solution to the reservoir and pH/EC monitoring.

Drill another hole in the covering of reservoir to pass a nutrient supply hose in the center of both towers.

Place a submersible pump in the center of the reservoir and attach the nutrient supply hose to the outlet of the pump.

Place a T barb on the nutrient supply hose at the same height as the tower to supply nutrient solution to both towers.

Place a timer to turn the pump on and off. The intervals for watering may depend on type of crop grown in the tower. For example, watering for lettuce can be continuous for 24 hours, while for strawberries, the recommended watering is seven to 10 times per day for one hour.

Place the net pot into a net pot hole, place some expanded clay balls or other media into it, and place the plant over these balls. Also, fill clay balls around the plant.

Start the pump. If you see the water splashing out of the pot, it may wet the leaves of plants. This can lead to fungal diseases and may cause death of the plant. To avoid this, take an aluminum sheet and cut a shield of the same size as the template for the water splash shield given at the end using the link listed under the template on the last page. Stick this shield near the pot hole opening above the clay balls

This keeps the plant from being splashed from the nutrient solution.

Strawberry plant with water splash shield on it.

97

Provide a support to the tower from the top using some wire or a bar.

Post preparation care

Avoid water leakage.

Clean tower with bleach after each round of crop.

Monitoring of pH and EC for solution according to crop grown. Water level in tank should be maintained.

CONCLUSION

A tower garden includes an A-Frame hydroponic system, hydroponic wall and cascades of bottles. It can be used for growing various crops like strawberry, lettuce, Swiss chard, herbs, spinach, kale, broccoli and flowering petunia. There are various online sources to get these systems, which can cost around $500 or more, but you can build your own tower garden for much less. It can also be used for growing plants indoors if lights are provided above the tower, which is popular in urban areas with only a small space for gardening. The tower garden design described here can hold 28 plants per tower and two towers can be placed in a 5-foot x 5-foot space, producing 56 plants at one time (Figure 1). The design can be modified according to preference. For example, towers can be hung from the top and can drain to a single tank to collect the nutrient solution. Materials listed below can be found at a hardware store, except the net pots which can be purchased from hydroponic dealers or online. If tower material is modified, make sure to use food grade material.